Why Living Things Need...

# Water

Daniel Nunn

**www.raintreepublishers.co.uk**
Visit our website to find out more information about Raintree books.

**To order:**
☎ Phone 0845 6044371
▤ Fax +44 (0) 1865 312263
✉ Email myorders@raintreepublishers.co.uk

Customers from outside the UK please telephone +44 1865 312262

Raintree is an imprint of Capstone Global Library Limited, a company incorporated in England and Wales having its registered office at 7 Pilgrim Street, London, EC4V 6LB – Registered company number: 6695582

Edited by Dan Nunn, Rebecca Rissman, and Sian Smith
Designed by Joanna Hinton-Malivoire
Picture research by Ruth Blair
Production by Victoria Fitzgerald
Originated by Capstone Global Library Ltd
Printed and bound in China by Leo Paper Products Ltd

ISBN 978 1 4062 3375 9
15 14 13 12 11
10 9 8 7 6 5 4 3 2 1

**British Library Cataloguing in Publication Data**
Nunn, Daniel.
 Why living things need... water.
 1. Water–Juvenile literature.
 I. Title
 553.7-dc22

**Acknowledgements**
We would like to thank the following for permission to reproduce photographs: Corbis pp.6 (© Yevgen Timashov/beyond), 7 (© Tetra Images), 9 (© Dale Spartas), 17 (© Ann & Steve Toon/Robert Harding World Imagery), 20 (© Wolfgang Kaehler); Getty Images pp.11 (Dave King/Dorling Kindersley), 14 (Peter Dazeley), 16 (Zak Kendal/Photonica), 21 (Ariel Skelley/Blend Images); Shutterstock pp.4 (© Dmitriy Shironosov), 5 (© Zurijeta ), 8 (© Dean Mitchell), 10 (© Villiers Steyn), 11 (© ronstik), 12 (© Willyam Bradberry), 13 (© Specta), 15 (© evan66), 18 (© beerkoff), 19 (© Gyukli Gyula), 22 (© Voyagerix), 22 (© Levent Konuk), 22 (© Ludmila Yilmaz), 23 (© Dmitriy Shironosov), 23 (© Villiers Steyn), 23 (© ronstik).

Front cover photograph of zebras reproduced with permission of Shutterstock (© Johan Swanepoel). Back cover photograph of a plant reproduced with permission of Shutterstock (© Gyukli Gyula).

We would like to thank Nancy Harris, Dee Reid, and Diana Bentley for their assistance in the preparation of this book.

Every effort has been made to contact copyright holders of material reproduced in this book. Any omissions will be rectified in subsequent printings if notice is given to the publisher.

# Contents

# What is water?

Water is a liquid. Liquids are runny.

Water has no smell, colour, or taste.

cloud

Water falls from the clouds as rain.

Rain fills up rivers, lakes, and oceans.

# Living things and water

People, other animals, and plants are living things.

All living things need water.

Animals drink water through
their mouths.

roots

Plants take in water through
their roots.

Some living things live in water.

Fish live in water.

# Why do living things need water?

People and other animals need water to stay alive.

Plants need water to stay alive, too.

People need water to keep their
bodies working.

Other animals need water to keep their bodies working, too.

Plants need water, air, and sunlight to make food.

Plants need water to grow.

Some living things use water to keep clean.

People use water to keep clean.

# Water quiz

Which of these things does not need water?

Answer on page 24

# Picture glossary

 **liquid** something runny that you can pour, such as water or milk

 **living thing** something that is alive, such as an animal or a plant

 **roots** the part of a plant that holds it in the ground. Roots bring water to the plant.

# Index

**Answer to question on page 22**
The fish and the tiger need water.
The books do not need water.

**Notes for parents and teachers**

**Before reading**

Take in a jug of water and show the children how you can easily pour the water into another container. Explain that water is a liquid and is runny. Can they think of another liquid that they can drink that is runny? Pass the water round and ask the children if it has a smell. Does it have a colour? Ask the children to take a small mouthful of water from their own water containers and ask if they think it has a taste. Explain that all living things need water to stay alive.

**After reading**

• Set up an area where small groups can pour water from one container to another. Ask them why they can do this. Encourage the use of vocabulary such as "liquid" and "runny".

• Provide two small potted plants. Explain that one plant will be given a little water every day but the other plant will not get any water. At the end of the week show the children the plants and ask them what has happened. With the help of the children write up the experiment onto a large sheet of paper. Ask two children to illustrate the results.